The London Book

W0372009

Titles in this series:

Level 1

Dear Mary Ann
Carol Christian

Kidnap in the Outback
Stella Martin

Fish and Chips and other adventures
David Couper

The Bus
Richard Hughes

Young Detective
John Escott

Crime Stories
Francis Radice

Where is Paula?
Diana Mitchener

Level Two

Switch On: Computers
Keith Hose

Pony Trek Adventure
Diana Mitchener

Mystery Tales
Francis Radice

Royal Court Hotel
Patty Key and Stephen Kirby

In Search of Happiness
David Couper

The Big Heat
Peter Buckley

The Professor is Missing
Caroline Reading

The Treasure of Hamilton Hall
Elizabeth Bencze

Level Three

Disco Blues
David Couper

Popular Jokes in English
George Woolard

Tuesday the Tenth
Joc Potter and Andy Hopkins

Alison's Revenge
Stella Martin

The House in the Hollow
Donn Byrne

Have I Passed?
Peter Buckley

Level 4

The Offa Trail
Sylvia Moody

Adventure in Hong Kong
Stella Martin

The Hot Seat and other stories
Donn Byrne

False Accusation
Richard Hughes

Soap Opera – The Reader
Charlyn Wessels and others

The London Book
Michael Vaughan-Rees

The Greenpeace Effect
Patrick Hurley

Appearance and Reality
David Maule

Tropical Rainforests
Stella Martin

The London Book

Michael Vaughan-Rees

MACMILLAN
PUBLISHERS

© Text Michael Vaughan-Rees 1991
© Illustrations Macmillan Publishers Ltd 1991

All rights reserved. No reproduction, copy or transmission of this publication may be made without written permission.

No paragraph of this publication may be reproduced, copied or transmitted save with written permission or in accordance with the provisions of the Copyright, Designs and Patents Act 1988, or under the terms of any licence permitting limited copying issued by the Copyright Licensing Agency, 33-4 Alfred Place, London, WC1E 7DP.

Any person who does any unauthorised act in relation to this publication may be liable to criminal prosecution and civil claims for damages.

First published 1991

Published by
MACMILLAN PUBLISHERS LIMITED
London and Basingstoke

Typeset by Macmillan Production Limited

Printed in Singapore

A CIP catalogue record for this book is available from the British Library

ISBN 0-333 53400-X

The author and publishers wish to acknowledge, with thanks, the following photographic sources:
Camera Press; Mary Evans Picture Library; Hulton-Deutsch Collection; Topham Picture Library.

The publishers have made every effort to trace the copyright holders, but if they have inadvertently overlooked any, they will be pleased to make the necessary arrangements at the first opportunity.

Cover and inside artwork by George Craig

Contents

Introduction

The London Book offers a lively and up-to-date description of Britain's capital city; a description that shows not only a 'guidebook' London, but the London of the people who actually live and work there.

The first part, *London's Past*, gives an historical perspective on the development of modern London.

The kinds of things people today like to do and see are described in *London's Pleasures*. This is not only a useful guide for the visitor, but also an informative glimpse of the kind of pleasures and entertainment Londoners enjoy.

London People reflects the cosmopolitan, multicultural face of the city. Today's Londoner may well be a recent immigrant, or the child of first- or second-generation immigrants and they talk here of their own experiences in coming to, and settling in, the city.

In *London Changes*, some of the city's older inhabitants describe the changes they have seen in their own lifetimes. Different relationships and lifestyles in a modern society, changes in industry and trade, have all had an effect. Now, huge new developments are changing the face of the city. How do Londoners feel about their new city?

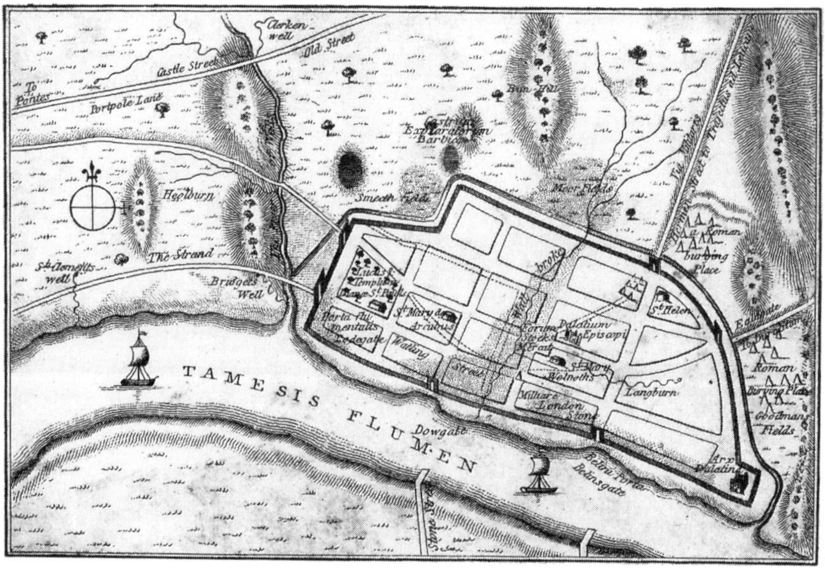

Roman London

Part 1: London Past

Roman London AD 43-400

When Julius Caesar invaded Britain in the year 55 BC there were probably no people living in what is now London. But about one hundred years later – according to experts at the Museum of London – the troops of the Emperor Claudius would have found an organised, man-made landscape, possibly with Iron Age huts and villages.

Claudius's commander, Aulus Plautus, built the first bridge across the Thames, just a few yards downstream of the present London Bridge. Within a few years the small town of Londinium became an important trading centre.

It was a good place to choose – not too far from the coast and situated on a tidal river, which meant that ships could come straight in from the sea. The south bank was flat and marshy then, so they started building on the north bank, probably using the twin hills of St Paul's and Cornhill for the first fortifications.

The native inhabitants of Britain, the Celts, were not prepared to accept the Roman presence, however. In AD 61 Queen Boudicca (Boadicea), of the Iceni tribe, led an attack on London in which many thousands of people were killed and the town itself was completely destroyed. But the Romans did not want to abandon such an important centre, and the new Governor began a major rebuilding programme, including an amphitheatre, public baths and a beautiful palace for the Governor himself. The remains of the palace are now two or three hundred metres from the river, but in the first century the river was much wider

– up to a kilometre across at high tide – and the palace was originally right on the river bank.

During the next 150 years other great buildings were erected. The most important of these were a forum (public square) and a basilica (town hall) – the largest north of the Alps – and an even bigger fort, at Cripplegate, set in the north-west corner of the wall which the Romans built right round the town. (You can trace the line of the wall if you join up the various gates whose names survive today – Ludgate, Newgate, Aldersgate, Cripplegate, Bishopsgate and Aldgate.) There was no need for a wall on the river side, of course, and recent excavations have uncovered a complete Roman waterfront.

Not many of these remains survive, unfortunately. You can see part of the Roman Wall near the Museum of London and there is a reconstruction of the Temple of Mithras (a Persian sun-god, popular with soldiers) in Queen Victoria Street. But Roman sites are continually being discovered, and more will certainly be preserved and opened to visitors in years to come.

After the Romans AD 400-1100

In the early fifth century the Romans abandoned Britain, and the town of London fell into ruins. The next settlers, the Saxons, preferred to build simple, wooden houses on the open land to the west of the walls. But in the ninth century a more dangerous type of invader, the Vikings, started to arrive. During one raid, in 851, over three hundred Danish ships sailed up the Thames and burned down the town. As a result of this, the Saxon King Alfred ordered his people to reoccupy the ancient city within the walls. From then on, and for many hundreds of years to come, few Londoners lived outside what had been the Roman city.

For two hundred years it was here that the various kings of England lived. But, in the eleventh century, King Edward (the Confessor) moved to a new royal palace, close to where Westminster Abbey was being built. Edward died in January 1066 and his successor, Harold, was the first king of England to be crowned in the new Abbey. Harold, too, died within a few months, killed at the Battle of Hastings, and the leader of the Norman invaders, William the Conqueror, was himself crowned king of England in the Abbey on Christmas Day 1066.

William began building the Tower of London to the east of the city wall, though he continued to live in the new Palace of Westminster. Since then, there has been a strict division between the City of London – the commercial and financial centre, known simply as 'the City' – and Westminster, the centre of government.

The Middle Ages and the Tudor period

By the time that Henry VIII came to the throne in 1509, the population of London had grown to about 50,000. The majority lived in the narrow streets and alleys of the City, still within the Roman and medieval walls. Most of the rest, connected with the Court or the Church, lived near the Abbey or the Palace at Westminster.

Much of the land was owned by the Church. In and around the City were dozens of monasteries and convents where the members of religious orders (monks and nuns) lived, many of them doing the things which are now organised by the state: running hospitals, schools, and homes for the old and the poor, for example.

Outside the City, most of what is now the West End of London was Church property, too. It was mainly farmland at that time, but the richest Churchmen chose to live on the best sites. Various bishops had fine palaces set in huge gardens along the north bank of the Thames, while the Bishops of Winchester and Rochester owned most of the south bank. Richest of all was the Archbishop of York whose palace was so magnificent that King Henry took it

The Globe Theatre in the days of Shakespeare

away from him and turned it into Whitehall Palace for his own use.

In fact the King, after quarrelling with the Pope, finally closed down the monasteries and took over all the Church's land. He kept most of this land for himself, and gave the rest to his friends. The names of some of these new landowners are familiar to anyone who knows the streets and squares of London – Bedford, Southampton, Arundel, Portman – and their descendants still own large parts of the city.

So much land became available that the population of London had increased very quickly to 200,000 by the end of the sixteenth century. The various kings and queens were against development outside the walls, so the City soon became greatly overcrowded; people were crammed into each room, cheap houses were built on every open space, and extra floors were put on top of existing houses, sometimes almost touching the buildings on the other side of the narrow streets.

When the people of the City wanted to find amusement they often walked across the bridge to Southwark, where things were not quite so crowded. Much of the entertainment available was of a very low type; there were inns and brothels, as well as places where people paid to see bulls and bears attacked by fighting dogs. But it was here, too, that the great Elizabethan theatres were to be found, including Shakespeare's Globe, opened in 1599, and the earlier, smaller Rose (the site of which has recently been discovered).

All the theatres in London were closed down in the 1640s when the Puritans came to power at the time of the Civil War. When theatre-going became popular again in the 1660s, following the Restoration of the Stuart monarchy, it was on the north bank that the theatres were built.

Just before the Civil War, one of the first great developments took place, when the Earl of Bedford was allowed to build on his land in Long Acre and Covent (formerly 'Convent') Garden. The Earl was lucky in his choice of architect. Inigo Jones had studied in Italy, and the influence of the Italian style can be seen in his major works, which include the Banqueting Hall in Whitehall and the Queen's House in Greenwich. When it came to Covent Garden he decided to build an Italian-style piazza (square) with the fine new church of St Paul on one side and great houses on the other three sides. It was an immediate success and rich families rushed to buy up all the houses. Not surprisingly, when similar developments were again allowed after the Restoration, squares became the favoured place of residence for those who could afford to live in style. There would be little or no through traffic; a leafy garden could be planted in the centre; horses and carriages could be kept in the private 'mews' running behind the houses. Small wonder that the London squares remained popular with the upper classes throughout the rest of the century and for the next two hundred years.

The Restoration and the Great Fire

The main reason that the great landowners gave for wanting to develop their estates was that people needed to be able to breathe fresh country air, as far away as possible from the City. To the north of Covent Garden, the Earl of Southampton turned his farmland into what became Bloomsbury. Meanwhile, to the west, Henry Jermyn, the Duke of St Albans, was developing the area around St James's. King Charles II himself improved three of the Royal Parks, St James's in particular, planting it with trees and stocking it with animals and birds.

Fresh air was certainly needed. Throughout the Middle Ages the City had known a series of attacks of the deadly disease known as 'the plague'. Then, in 1665, came the Great Plague during which thousands of people died. It was clearly time to do something about the dreadful conditions. But the Plague was followed in 1666 by the Great Fire, which destroyed some eighty per cent of the City, including 89 churches and St Paul's Cathedral.

Within days, the great Christopher Wren had drawn up a plan for a completely new type of City, with wide avenues and spacious piazzas. But so many of the landowners needed to start up their businesses again that rebuilding work began, using the old street plans. The new City differed in two ways from the old, however. Firstly, Wren was asked to design a new cathedral as well as dozens of churches; secondly, strict new rules were introduced to control the materials and style of all new buildings.

But not everyone wanted to go back to the City. Within a few years new suburbs had sprung up outside the ancient walls, each housing different types of tradespeople; tailors, jewellers, gold- and silversmiths, for example. And the westward march continued as land and property fell into the hands of the new king's favourites; the Earl of LEICESTER, Sir Thomas BOND, Henry COVENTRY, Lord BERKELEY. The proudest of these was George Villiers, Duke of Buckingham; and before his land was sold he insisted that every part of his name should be included in the various street names. To this day, near Charing Cross, you will find not only GEORGE Court, VILLIERS Street and BUCKINGHAM Street, but if you look carefully in York Place (just off Villiers Street) you will see the words 'formerly OF Alley'.

The eighteenth century

The Stuart monarchy came to an end in 1714 with the death of Queen Anne. Three years later, the family of her successor, George I, was celebrated in the name of Hanover Square, one of the few truly baroque squares in London. Other developments took place further south, especially around Piccadilly, where Lord Burlington gave his name to three different streets.

Meanwhile, the new suburbs needed churches, and these were begun following the famous 1710 Act for the Building of Fifty Churches. Not all fifty were built, but the Act

Leicester Square in 1753

brought about some of London's greatest churches, including St George's in Hanover Square, St Martin-in-the-Fields (on the east side of Trafalgar Square), St Mary-le-Strand, and St John's in Smith Square (now a concert hall).

Wren was still busy rebuilding St Paul's Cathedral, but one of his former assistants, Nicholas Hawksmoor, was responsible for six of the churches: Christchurch, Spitalfields; St-George-in-the-East; St Anne's, Limehouse; St Mary Woolnoth; St George's, Bloomsbury and St Alphege, Greenwich. All are masterpieces (though some have been damaged and restored) and all are worth visiting.

The eighteenth century has, in fact, been described as the 'golden age' of architecture in London. The ancient City gates were demolished in 1760, symbolising the fact that the Middle Ages were long in the past. The following year, the Lighting and Paving Act made the main streets cleaner and brighter than those of any city in Europe. More of the great squares were built, including perhaps the finest in all of London, BEDFORD SQUARE (still belonging to the same family since the time of Henry VIII). And even more names were added to the map of London. The village of Chelsea was developed by Sir Hans Sloane and his son-in-law, Charles Cadogan. The Grosvenors were scattering their family names south of Oxford Street while, to the north, a vast estate was developed by Edward Harley, Baron Wigmore. (Not content with HARLEY and WIGMORE streets, he named MORTIMER and DE VERE streets after his other titles, HENRIETTA Street and CAVENDISH Square after his wife, MARGARET Street after his daughter, while HOLLES and WIMPOLE streets commemorate his wife's father.)

This was the age of elegance, with fashionable London meeting at the beautiful new Royal Opera House, opened in Covent Garden in 1732, or dining and dancing in the public pleasure gardens of Vauxhall and Ranelagh.

But not all of London was well-paved and brightly lit. Poor families crowded into every little space, and the courts and alleys off St Martin's Lane, St Giles and the Strand housed a mass of people trying to earn a living in any way possible. If there was not enough to eat they could always drink to forget their hunger. Gin was the most popular drink of the working class, and the saying was 'Drunk for a penny, dead drunk for tuppence' [= two pence]. Even the wide streets such as the Haymarket were full of prostitutes, while the parks were dangerous after dark and far from safe during the day.

One group of people who found it more difficult to get work in the second half of the eighteenth century were the 'watermen'. From Roman times until well into the nineteenth century, the river was the easiest way to transport both goods and people about London, and it was the watermen who rowed the passenger boats. They were the taxi-drivers of their time, and during the second half of the sixteenth century there were some 3,000 working between London Bridge and Westminster alone. Their only competition was from the 'horse-ferry' at Westminster, owned by the Archbishop of Canterbury, where a horse and coach could be carried across on a flat boat. (Horseferry Road shows where the ferry used to be.)

In 1751 a second bridge over the Thames was built, at Westminster, with Blackfriars Bridge following in 1769. The watermen were paid a sum of money in compensation (though not as much as the Archbishop, who received the enormous sum of £3,000). And from then on the number of watermen dropped every year, as more bridges were built, the streets were improved, and other forms of public transport became popular.

The nineteenth century

In the first quarter of the following century, three more bridges were built between Westminster and the City; Vauxhall, Waterloo and Southwark. The main result of this was that the south bank became easier to reach and soon filled up with cheap, working-class terraced housing.

On the other side of the river more prestigious developments were taking place. George, Prince of Wales, became Prince Regent in 1811 and engaged John Nash to draw up plans for his own property. St James's Park was given the shape it has today and the future king created another royal park – Regent's Park – from his own lands in the Marylebone area. Through the north of the park runs the Regent's Canal, while Regent Street was at the centre of Nash's imaginative scheme for joining the Park to The Mall.

But it was the coming of the railways in the period 1836-1876 which did most to change the face of London. About 100,000 people were thrown out of their homes as the railway lines moved in towards the centre (700 houses were destroyed in Waterloo alone when the line was extended from Nine Elms). The main effect, however, was on the distance people could now travel between their home and their place of work. Until the coming of the railway most people lived within walking distance of their work. But as the lines spread outwards into the countryside, it became normal to live in the suburbs and travel in to the centre every day. At first it was only the middle classes who moved out, but the railways soon introduced cheap 'workmen's tickets' to encourage everyone to take the train.

The movement towards the suburbs became even more important from 1890 onwards with the opening of the first electric underground line (or 'tube'). And as the population of the suburbs increased, that of the City fell. In 1801 London had a population of about 959,000, of whom 120,000 lived in the City. A hundred years later there were some 4.5 million people living in Greater London, but only 30,000 in the City.

This does not mean that no building took place in central London. Much of the central slum area was pulled down as new wide streets were built or existing streets widened. The biggest building operation of all was the construction of the Embankment along the north side of the Thames.The first

The construction of the Embankment, near the Houses of Parliament

part ran from Chelsea to Millbank (near the Tate Gallery). Then in the 1870s, the Victoria Embankment, extending from Westminster to Blackfriars, was built. The quickest way to get from the City to Westminster had always been by boat. Now, the days of the Thames as the main London highway were over.

The twentieth century

The story of London in our own century is one of construction, destruction and reconstruction. More villages and green fields were swallowed up as what has been called the 'urban sprawl' carried on, especially in the twenties and thirties, as motor cars, buses and new underground lines made it even easier to live far out and 'commute' into the centre. The countryside was disappearing so fast, in fact, that in 1937 the London County Council proposed a 'Green Belt' area around London to limit the extent of urban development.

Within London itself there had been another building boom, with some 250,000 properties going up in the years from 1920-30. Many large properties in the centre disappeared, to be replaced by blocks of luxury flats, hotels, department stores and other commercial premises.

With the coming of war in 1939, practically all building stopped. Then, in September 1940, the first of the German bombs fell on London. Night after night for months on end, the 'Blitz' went on, with the docklands, the East End and the City the worst-hit places. In June 1944 the attacks started up again, this time using the V-1 and V-2 rockets. By the end of the war, well over 100,000 houses in the London area had been destroyed and a further million damaged by bombing or rocket attack. Over a third of the City lay in ruins, though St Paul's had managed to survive.

It took many years before the ruins were cleared away and rebuilding started. And there are few people – apart from the architects responsible, perhaps – who are happy

London, April 1942, after the 'Blitz'. St Paul's had managed to survive

with what has been built. If you look at pictures of the City from any time between, say, 1700 and 1940, you see a skyline dominated by St Paul's Cathedral, with the spires of the other Wren churches standing out proudly. Now, the remaining churches are lost among anonymous office blocks, and even St Paul's looks unhappy hiding among the new buildings.

It was even worse for the families who had lost their homes in the Blitz. They were used to living in friendly, old terraced streets, where everybody knew everybody else; many were now put into ugly 'high-rise' blocks, cut off from each other and surrounded by wasteland.

In 1959, the Royal Fine Art Commission referred to the 'drabness' and 'mediocrity' of much modern inner-city architecture and to the 'deplorably low standard' of what was being built, especially in London. In June of the following year, planners from the London County Council tried to set up a series of rules controlling the spread of high-rise buildings. But there was so much money to be made from property development that great pressure was put on local authorities to approve planning applications. The results can be seen all around the city; the Shell Centre on the South Bank, Centrepoint on the corner of Oxford Street and Tottenham Court Road; the list is too depressingly long to complete.

In 1984, Prince Charles asked, 'Why has everything got to be vertical, straight, unbending and functional?'; and in recent years many people – including some architects – have shared his feelings. 'Post-modernist' buildings, and others built in imitations of much older styles, are becoming increasingly popular. And ordinary people are now prepared to fight in order to prevent massive redevelopment – something that will be looked at again in the last chapter.

Part 2: London Pleasures

In this chapter, you will find some suggestions for ways of enjoying yourself in London without having to spend a lot of money. And I intend to include places where you are likely to meet Londoners, rather than just other tourists.

Not that you should always avoid doing things that tourists traditionally do. The National Gallery, for example, is a must for any lover of painting. But don't go there at 11.30 in the morning; you will hardly be able to move for the crowds. What you should do is study a plan of the gallery, arrive at 9.50am (ten minutes before opening time), then walk fairly fast to the room you're most interested in (don't run or the attendants will be very worried); that way, you will probably have ten minutes all alone before anyone else arrives.

And don't say to yourself, 'I won't go on the river, because the boats are full of tourists when the sun is shining'. Of course they are! There are few better ways to spend a sunny day in London than to go on the river. But why not try it when the weather looks bad? I recently took a boat from Westminster upstream to Hampton Court Palace. It had rained earlier in the morning and there were no more than twenty of us on a boat built for two hundred. This was the very same journey that Henry VIII often used to make after he had taken the Palace over from Cardinal Wolsey, the Lord Chancellor (it had not been wise to build a finer palace than anything owned by the king!). Henry travelled in the royal barge rowed by watermen in uniforms of red and gold, spending the night at Syon House, about half-way. Our trip was rather shorter, lasting a pleasant three hours. During the two or three showers, we just went below for a coffee or beer and looked out through the windows till the rain stopped. We passed under twenty bridges – which would have been a surprise for Henry, as would the Houses of Parliament, Battersea Power Station and much else besides. But he would have recognised every bend and island on the river; and the long straight stretch between Kew and Isleworth has hardly changed since his time. Herons still sit on the branches of the trees watching for fish, which the Thames is now clean enough to provide.

Student cards

If you are studying in England, then see if you can have a student card. It can often get you reductions and discounts, especially to exhibitions and theatres.

Transport

London has an extensive bus, rail and underground system. (The only part of London not properly served by underground is the south-east, but you can reach places such as Greenwich and Blackheath by rail from Charing Cross or Waterloo East.)

If you are staying for a while, it is usually best to buy a weekly or monthly pass. (You will need a passport-size photograph.) If you want to travel a lot around the London area at weekends or after 9.30am during the week, buy a one-day travel card from a railway station. You can use it on the railway, underground and bus system.

When there are three or four of you then it is worth taking a taxi. It will still be a bit more expensive than public transport (and the driver will expect a 10-15% tip) but it can save a great deal of time and frustration.

Finally, it is worth thinking of using the river as a way of getting from A to B instead of just as a pleasure trip. In the summer you can travel upstream, to Kew or Richmond. Downstream services operate all year round, from Westminster and Charing Cross to the Tower of London and Greenwich. And the development of the Docklands area has meant that a new riverbus service, the Thames Line, now runs between Chelsea and Docklands, stopping on the way at such places as the South Bank (by the Festival Hall) and London Bridge.

Walks

Why not buy a good map and try walking? That's the cheapest way of all, and you can always combine it with other forms of transport. Here are a few of my favourite walks, both in the centre and farther out.

A canal walk

London isn't Venice or Bruges, but it does have an extensive system of canals. The place where canals can change levels is called a 'lock' and there is a huge, popular market at Camden Lock on Saturdays and Sundays. Take the underground to Camden Town (Northern Line) then follow the crowds. There is everything from cheap clothes to bric-a-brac and antiques, with plenty of food available. Then you can walk westwards along the Regent's Canal, through Regent's Park and the north part of London Zoo to Little Venice (Warwick Road tube).

Just before Lisson Grove, the canal path stops and you have to come up to street level. If it's Saturday and you haven't had enough of markets, go to Church Street; as well as a general market, there's a big building called Alfie's with fifty or sixty excellent antique shops. (Note: if you don't feel like walking, you can take a canal boat

Camden Lock market

from Camden Lock to Little Venice, or the other way round.)

Highgate and Hampstead

This walk takes you to two parts of north London which still have a village feel about them. Take the underground to Highgate (Northern Line). Cross the busy Archway Road and walk up Jackson's Lane to Highgate Village. If you are interested in painting you should walk along Hampstead Lane to Kenwood House, a beautiful seventeenth-century mansion remodelled by Robert Adam in the 1760s. It contains a fine collection of paintings (Rembrandt, Vermeer, Gainsborough, etc.) and entrance is free. Alternatively, for something rather different, walk down Swains Lane to Highgate Cemetery and visit the extraordinary grave of Karl Marx, then carry on down the Lane to Parliament Hill. Both of these routes take you to different parts of Hampstead Heath, a piece of countryside rather than a park, from the highest point of which you have superb views over London. After you have strolled about the Heath you can explore Hampstead itself.

By now, you will need to sit down for a while, so you can either visit the Everyman, one of the oldest independent cinemas in London, or Louis' for tea or coffee and superb pastries.

Greenwich

Another splendid view over London, but from the south-east this time, is from the top of the oldest of the royal parks, at Greenwich. The best way to approach the park is to take the train to Blackheath, turn left out of the station and follow the road round through the village till you get to the Heath itself. Cross the Heath and you reach the gate into the park. Walk down Blackheath Avenue to the Old Royal Observatory, centred on a house built by Wren in 1675. The zero line of longitude runs through the grounds, so you can stand with one foot in the western hemisphere and the other in the eastern.

Below the Observatory is the National Maritime Museum, the central part of which – the Queen's House – was designed by Inigo Jones. Between the Museum and the river is the Royal Naval College, on which three of the greatest British architects worked; Wren himself, with Hawksmoor as assistant, followed by Sir John Vanbrugh (designer of Blenheim Palace and a successful writer of plays).

All of these buildings are open to the public, as is the Cutty Sark, a beautiful 'Tea Clipper', that is to say, a sailing ship which was used to carry tea from India in the 1870s.

River boats leave regularly from the nearby pier, heading upstream to Charing Cross, Tower and Westminster Piers. Or you can walk *under* the river to the Isle of Dogs. If you are tired of walking by now, the Docklands Light Railway will take you as far as the Tower of London (weekdays only, at the time of writing).

Legal London

Until the eighteenth century, law students both lived and studied in one of the four Inns of Court; Lincoln's Inn, the Inner Temple, the Middle Temple and Gray's Inn. Nowadays, these quiet lanes and courtyards contain the 'chambers', that is to say, the offices, of practising lawyers – both *barristers*, who appear in the upper courts, and *solicitors*, who instruct or 'brief' the barristers on behalf of their clients.

Starting from Holborn station (Central Line), turn left into Kingsway then left again into Remnant Street. This brings you to Lincoln's Inn Fields, laid out as public gardens by Inigo Jones himself. Jones is said to have designed the oldest house on the square, number 59-60, in about 1640, though most of the houses date from the following century. These include number 13, reconstructed in 1792 by the architect Sir John Soane, and now one of the most delightful museums in London.

Walk through the central gardens to the east side of the square and (on weekdays) you will be able to enter Lincoln's Inn itself. The Inn has been here since at least 1422 and the Old Hall dates from1489. The chapel is said to have been rebuilt by Inigo Jones and the Hall and Library are early Victorian, with other buildings of all periods in between. You will see the names of the occupants of the various chambers painted on boards at the foot of the staircases, a custom also to be found in many of the colleges of Oxford and Cambridge.

To the south, you come into Carey Street (from which comes the expression 'to be in Queer Street', meaning 'to be bankrupt'). From here you can take the back way into the Royal Courts of Justice. Alternatively, turn left, then right into Chancery Lane. This leads to Fleet Street, which used to be the headquarters of the national press till all the newspapers moved into new, high-tech buildings; you can still see the former *Express* and *Telegraph* offices, good examples of late 1920's architecture.

On the south side of Fleet Street, almost opposite Chancery Lane, is the fine seventeenth-century entrance to the Middle Temple. This was originally the headquarters of the Knights Templar until they were abolished in 1312. Parts of the oldest building in the complex, the Temple church, date from the time of the Templars, but most come from the sixteenth and seventeenth centuries.

The Temple is an oasis of peace and quiet, a good place to rest for a while after a long day's sightseeing or shopping. When you feel you should move on, take one of the two lanes heading south to the Victoria Embankment. Turn right to Temple underground, or left to Blackfriars.

Sitting down

Here are some other places where you can get away from the crowds.

- The **Royal Parks**, of course. Especially St James's Park (by the lake); around the Serpentine in Hyde Park; anywhere in Kensington Gardens or Regent's Park.
- **Victoria Tower Gardens**, just west of the Houses of Parliament, overlooking the river.
- **Golden Square**, just off Brewer Street, right in the heart of Soho.
- **Victoria Embankment Gardens**, by Embankment tube.
- **Russell Square**, north-east of the British Museum.
- **The Gardens**, Paddington Street, W1. This little garden, between Baker Street and Marylebone High Street, was St George's Burial Ground from 1731–1857, which might explain why it is so peaceful and undisturbed.
- **Archbishops Park**, next to Lambeth Place. Cross Lambeth Bridge, walk down Lambeth Road and take a little alley on your left to find an almost deserted green space, tennis courts and all.
- Finally, you might welcome the little gardens in **Mayfair** between Mount Street, Farm Street and South Audley Street (by the Church of the Immaculate Conception).

Looking down

For those of you not afraid of heights, you can try the following places:

- **Tower Bridge**: a lift will take you right up to the top, for spectacular views of the Tower of London and the new developments on the South Bank.
- **The Monument**: designed by Wren to commemorate the Great Fire, this is the tallest isolated stone column in the world (311 steps).
- **St Paul's Cathedral**: climb up to the Stone Gallery for one of the best views over the City.

St James's Park

Film

Some West End cinemas are cheaper on Monday evenings. Local cinemas are usually cheaper than the West End, so check the programmes there.

Look in the weekly magazine *Time Out* for details of cinemas which show a wider selection of films than the ones just mentioned. Seats are generally cheaper than in the West End and most have student reductions. Cheap French films are shown at the French Institute (17 Queensbury Place, SW7) and the Centre Charles Peguy (16 Leicester Square); the Goethe Institut (Princes Gate, SW7) shows German films.

The Barbican Cinema has student reductions and currently has a policy of selling four tickets for the price of three.

The Museum of London (near the Barbican) shows classic British films for less than half of the prices at cinemas.

The National Film Theatre (Waterloo) has student membership available by the year or by the week. Unsold tickets and a few 'standby' tickets are available at a reduced price half an hour before the performance. And if you are a member of the NFT you have reduced entry to the adjacent Museum of the Moving Image, the most exciting new museum in London (certainly for anyone interested in the history of the cinema and television). The layout of the museum is chronological, so you follow it round from the first attempts to represent movement, through the silent cinema and on to the present day. Children can try their hand at drawing cartoons, and anyone can have a go at seeing how good they are at reading the television news. Best of all, instead of the usual bored attendants, the museum employs actors who play roles appropriate to the part of the museum they are working in. So when you reach the '30s you may see an actress trying out some dance steps for a Hollywood musical, or a director rehearsing a scene from a cowboy film.

Museums and galleries

Not all museums are quite so lively, though many have things that you can touch and operate. Sadly, an increasing number of museums in London charge an entrance fee, including the Science, Geological and Natural History Museums in South Kensington. Note, however, that one ticket (half-price for students) allows you into both the Natural History and Geological Museums.

The best-known museums and galleries are very crowded, especially at weekends. So try some lesser-known ones. My favourites include three which reflect the taste of private collectors.

The Wallace Collection: Manchester Square, W1. (Bond Street tube.) Open Monday-Saturday 10am-5pm and Sunday 2-5pm. Especially good for seventeenth-century Dutch and eighteenth-century French painting. (I recommend: the two de Hooch interiors, the portrait of Madame de Pompadour by Boucher and 'The Swing' by Fragonard.)

Soane Museum: 13 Lincoln's Inn Fields, WC2. (Kingsway tube.) Open Tuesday-Saturday 10am-5pm. Sir John Soane was an architect and collector who designed this house for himself in 1812, and lived in it until his death in 1837. Its somewhat crowded contents include Hogarth's splendid 'Rake's Progress'.

Courtauld Institute Galleries: Somerset House, The Strand, WC2, near the north end of Waterloo Bridge. (Temple tube.) Open Monday-Saturday 10am-5pm and Sunday 2-5pm. Practically everything is of the highest quality, especially the French Impressionist and Post-Impressionist paintings. (Look out for Manet's painting 'Bar at the Folies Bergères'.) Not free, but definitely worth the price of admission (reduced, if you have a student card).

Many museums and galleries offer various free activities, which can include guided tours, lectures (talks) and film shows. As well as the three just mentioned check the following institutions:

The National Gallery in Trafalgar Square; **The National Portrait Gallery** (round the corner from the National Gallery, in St Martin's Place); **The Tate Gallery**, Millbank, for British art, and for modern art in general (Pimlico tube); **The Victoria and Albert Museum**, in South Kensington; **The British Museum**, Great Russell Street, as well as its ethnographic department, **The Museum of Mankind** in Burlington Gardens, just off Bond Street. And note that the National Gallery now stays open till 8pm on Wednesday evenings during June, July and August.

London is one of the great centres of the international art market, so you can see works of art in many commercial galleries. (The top ones are in and around Bond Street; others are in the Portobello/Ladbroke Grove area.) Also look out for student shows from May to July. This is when students of painting, ceramics, sculpture, etc. from the many art colleges exhibit the work they have done over the year. A good time to look out for future talent (and maybe buy before they have become established). Check details in the art section of *Time Out*.

Music

Classical, opera, ballet

The Royal Opera House (opera or ballet), Sadlers Wells (ballet) and the London Coliseum (English National Opera) all have day tickets on sale from 10am. And you *can* get regular cheap tickets. Unsold tickets are on sale cheaply, usually one hour before the performance. In July and August there are plenty of cheap tickets and a wealth of music at the 'Proms' (promenade concerts), held at the Royal Albert Hall in South Kensington.

Young musicians often give lunchtime concerts in the churches of the West End and the City, especially at St Martin-in-the-Fields (east side of Trafalgar Square).

The three top London music schools have regular free concerts by their students. Contact them for details if interested. (If you send them a stamped addressed envelope they will send you the programme for the term.)

The Royal College of Music, Prince Consort Road, SW7. Telephone (071) 823 8229.
The Royal Academy of Music, Marylebone Road, W1. Telephone (071) 935 5461
Trinity College, 11 Mandeville Place, W1, (behind Selfridges). Telephone (071) 935 5773

Rock, jazz, etc.
There are literally hundreds of places to dance or to listen to music, many of them small clubs and pubs where you can hear music for the price of a drink or a small admission charge. Check the *Time Out* music section.

Here are some of my favourite places to listen to jazz:

The Prince of Orange, 118 Lower Road, SE16. Till 12pm nightly and on Sunday lunchtimes.

The best jazz club in central London is Ronnie Scott's at 47 Frith Street in Soho. Monday to Thursday is cheaper than weekends. Reductions for students; massive reductions for members (but food and drink is not cheap).

Head up the river to the Bull's Head pub at Barnes, especially on summer evenings and at weekends.

At the Festival Hall on the South Bank there is free 'commuter jazz' from about 5.30pm to 7.30pm on Fridays. You can just sit down and listen, have a drink if you feel like it, or wander round one of the exhibitions.

South Bank

In fact, the South Bank arts complex offers a lot of free entertainment. The Festival Hall and National Theatre both have regular exhibitions. The Festival Hall has a programme of foyer music (classical, folk or jazz) every day from 12.30pm to 2pm. The National Theatre runs a similar programme before evening performances, from about 6pm to 7.45pm, also Saturdays from 1pm to 2.15pm. (The bars in both venues are pleasant, too.)

But it's nice just to stroll along the South Bank on a fine day, especially since they've started selling second-hand books from stalls in front of the National Film Theatre. And it's from here that you get the finest view of St Paul's.

Theatre

There are always a few shows which are permanently booked up. But do not think this necessarily means that they are any good! Tickets for other shows – many of them excellent – can often be bought cheaply at the Ticket Booth on the west side of Leicester Square. Entrance is half-price plus a reasonable booking fee. You can find out from *The Independent* which theatres still have plenty of tickets that day and be fairly certain that some will be available from the booth. (Opening times are 2.30pm–6.30pm for evening performances, 12.00pm–1.30pm for matinees.)

The National Theatre and the Royal Shakespeare Company (Barbican) have day tickets on sale cheaply from 10am. Get there early and you can even buy tickets for otherwise sold-out plays.

And don't forget previews, which usually cost two-thirds of the regular prices. (This is usually the week before the play officially opens.) Also, remember that matinees are cheaper than evening performances.

City institutions

Two of the great institutions in the City welcome visitors without charge.

The Bank of England Museum, Threadneedle Street, EC2R 8AH. Telephone (071) 601 5793.

The history of the Bank of England and its role today is shown through excellent exhibits with interactive video display. Pre-booked groups are offered a film show and a talk by a member of staff. From lst October to Easter it is open Monday to Friday 10am-6pm. In the summer season, it is also open on Saturdays as above and on Sundays from 2–6pm.

Lloyd's of London, Lime Street, EC3. Telephone (071) 327 6210.

This famous centre of international insurance is worth visiting for the building itself. Designed by Richard Rogers (of Pompidou Centre fame) it is vigorously modern, with lifts, stairways and pipes all on the outside. It is apparently much disliked by many of those who work there, but the view from the Visitor's Gallery down to the floor is breathtaking. Only prebooked groups are admitted and visits can be made during weekdays between 10am–12.30pm and 2.30–3.45pm.

Shopping

For really cheap second-hand clothes, books, etc. try charity shops. The best known are run by Oxfam and they are to be found all over London.

Look out also for jumble sales, often run by churches at

Lloyd's of London

weekends. (These are when people give things to the church, which are then sold for very little money.)

London has dozens of good second-hand clothes shops. For an amazing variety of American clothes try Flip (Long Acre, between Leicester Square and Covent Garden). For army surplus, hats, etc. try Laurence Corner (corner of Hampstead Road and Drummond Street, just off the Euston Road, Warren Street tube).

And look out for sales; they seem to go on all year round now.

Markets

Here are some more in addition to the ones mentioned earlier:

- The best-known East End market, Petticoat Lane, is held on Sundays in Middlesex Street, near Aldgate East tube. It specialises in cheap new clothes, things for the home, and so on. Five minutes away, just off Brick Lane, is the oldest flea market in London. The area is good for cheap Indian food, too.
- The longest market in London is along Portobello Road (Notting Hill Gate tube) on Saturdays. At Notting Hill it is all bric-a-brac and antiques, but as you go farther west it becomes cheaper until it ends up as a regular fruit and vegetable market, specialising in West Indian food.
- There are dozens of local markets for food and cheap clothing. The best retail food market is in Berwick Street (Soho). The food is fresh and cheap (and especially cheap at about 5pm in the evening).

Evening classes and community centres

Many foreign visitors say that they find it difficult to meet British people. Here are two suggestions for how to do so, especially if you are staying for a few months.

London has very many adult education institutes where you can take a wide variety of classes, from judo to art appreciation, from guitar lessons to vehicle maintenance. Most classes run for a year, but you can join many of them for a term. The fees are cheap, and details can be found in an annual publication called 'Floodlight' (available from most libraries).

Throughout London you will find community centres usually run by volunteers from the local area. The best ones (such as Jackson's Lane Community Centre in Highgate) have dozens of different activities; sport, drama, film-shows, youth clubs and so on. Find out from your local town hall which are the centres for your area. Everyone is welcome.

Food

I've already mentioned the food in the Brick Lane area on Sundays. You will find so-called 'Indian' restaurants all over Britain, though many are, in fact, run by people from Pakistan or Bangladesh. The menu will normally say how 'hot' a dish is. If not, ask the waiter to tell you.

Chinese restaurants are just as common as Indian, even in the suburbs. But best of all try the restaurants in Chinatown (Gerrard Street, Lisle Street, Wardour Street, near Leicester Square). Most serve Cantonese food, but you will find other regions represented. The liveliest time to be there is at Sunday lunchtime when the area is full of Chinese families, many trying the typical snacks called dim sum. These can be savoury or sweet, and they are either fried or steamed. Traditionally, they are pushed around on a trolley and you choose the ones you like the look of, but nowadays you often have to choose them from a menu (which can have illustrations to help you).
But there are dozens of other types of restaurants and

cafes, from all over the world. (You can even find English food if you look hard enough.) And why there is such a variety in London is something we will find out in the next chapter.

Part 3: London People

According to tradition, the only true Londoners are 'Cockneys', in other words those born within the sound of the 'Bow bells.' But nowadays, with London grown so large, there aren't many who can pass the ancient test of having been born close enough to the centre to hear the bells of St Mary-le-Bow church in Cheapside.

In fact, a Londoner today is just as likely to be from elsewhere in Europe, from a former British colony or, indeed, from anywhere in the world. And many of those born here in London are the children of first- or second-generation immigrants or can trace their ancestry back considerably earlier.

Take our friend Cecily, for example, now in her 60s:

> My maternal grandparents came over from Russia in the 1880s. He was a furrier and he was brought over to design furs for a model house here in London. He died quite early and I think it was because of chest complaints from working with all those furs all the time. Then my grandmother brought up seven children on her own, and she died very young, so my mother and her sisters and brothers were orphaned at a very early age and had to bring themselves up. The youngest was about two and the eldest girl about seventeen so she had to be the mother of the family, so to speak.

Cecily's grandparents lived in Spitalfields, one of the new suburbs developed just east of the City walls after the Great Fire. It had been associated with the cloth trade from the earliest days, having been settled by large numbers of

Asian immigrants arriving in London in 1968

Huguenot refugees from France, fleeing religious persecution in the late seventeenth century. Over the next hundred years it became the centre of the silk-weaving industry, and the great merchants built fine houses for themselves in the streets around Hawksmoor's Christchurch. But the weaving industry gradually declined and the various premises were taken over from the 1880s onwards by Jewish immigrants specialising in the clothing and fur trade, such as the employers of Cecily's grandfather.

This part of the East End has the occasional reminder of its Jewish past; the Spanish and Portuguese Synagogue in Bevis Street; the cheesecake and bagels; Bloom's restaurant in Whitechapel High Street with the best kosher food in London. But few of the workshops are Jewish owned nowadays. Instead they are, almost entirely, run by the latest immigrants to the area, Bengalis from the Sylhet region of what is now Bangladesh.

Raphael Samuel, in an article in the weekly *Spectator*, points out that the Bengalis 'seemed to re-enact the original pattern of Jewish settlement. They settled, most heavily, in the self-same streets. They took up the same trades. Like the Jews they formed, within their own precinct, an ethnic majority, treating the streets and pavements as communal spaces, and the shops and restaurants as meeting places.'

One of the buildings taken over by the Bengalis is the one on the corner of Fournier Street and Brick Lane which, more than anything else, serves as the symbol of the history of immigration in the area. Originally a church built in 1744 for the local Huguenot population, it was used as a synagogue from 1898 to 1975 and is now a mosque, serving the mainly Muslim Bengalis.

But not all those from the Indian sub-continent have settled in traditional immigrant areas. Southall, conveniently close to Heathrow Airport, has a population of whom some sixty per cent, mostly Punjabis, are of Asian origin; Wembley, on the other hand, has a large Gujarati population.

The Gujaratis are perhaps the most familiar of all London Asians, since they are actively involved in the retail trade. One such is Ashvin Patel, my local newsagent, whose family – like thousands of others – came to Britain not directly from Asia, but via Africa. His father, after service in the British Army, started work in 1946 as a foreman for a building firm in Kenya. Within ten years he had founded his own firm, rapidly becoming one of the top contractors in the country. Ashvin joined the firm in 1966, at the age of nineteen.

> As our business expanded throughout Kenya, it seemed a good idea to visit the various sites by plane, so I came to England in 1968 to study for my pilot's licence. By this time I was married – an arranged marriage according to our custom – and our first son was born here. But when I returned to Kenya the next year, I found the political climate changed. The country had been independent since 1963 and the policy of encouraging African businessmen meant that people like us with British passports had to apply for a work permit. My father died in 1971 and our work permits were not extended, nor were we allowed to have Kenyan citizenship. This meant that we had no choice but to leave everything behind and come to Britain, which we did in December 1972.
>
> There was no prospect of getting a job with an airline and I started work at the Ford Motor company in Dagenham on the assembly line. But friends gathered round and helped me buy a small shop. I sold up in 1976 and worked as a salesman for a while. Finally, last year, I bought this property here in Waterloo and transformed it into a proper confectionery and newsagents. And with the blessing of our Guru Shree Pramukh Swami Maharaj we have had little difficulty in increasing our turnover.

The main influx of East-African Asians – from Uganda as well as Kenya – was in the late 1960s and early '70s. Most immigrants coming directly from the Indian sub-continent arrived over the preceding ten years, a period which also saw the arrival of thousands of Cantonese-speaking Chinese from Hong Kong.

Chinese seamen had occasionally been seen in London from the late eighteenth century onwards, and by the end of the nineteenth century there was a small, permanent Chinese population in Limehouse serving the needs of the visitors. But much of the area was damaged during the Blitz or demolished for redevelopment in the post-war years. A few Chinese businesses had opened up meanwhile in the southern part of Soho, just north of Leicester Square. Now, it is hard to find a single business in the immediate area which is not Chinese-owned. But Chinese restaurants are found throughout London, one of the best being run by Mr Leung in Lee Green, close to the school where I work. He didn't start out in the restaurant business, however:

> No, back home in Hong Kong I was a printer. I worked for my father's business. But I wanted to see what life was like outside our country, so I came to England in 1963. I worked for someone else at first, in a restaurant in Nottingham. Then, after a while, I started a take-away business near Brighton and then I opened my own place here in 1981.
>
> My wife is from Hong Kong, too. She works in an insurance company. My brother-in-law is the chef here and my sister-in-law works here, too. It's good to have your family working with you. They pay more attention to the customers and more attention to the food.

An astonishing ninety per cent of the estimated 100,000 Chinese living in Britain are in the catering industry, with many of those working behind the scenes unable to speak a word of English, despite having lived here for many years.

This is not a problem faced by immigrants from the West Indies – since English is their mother tongue – though many of the older people have retained a strong accent and

The southern part of London's Soho district is now known as 'Chinatown' because of the large Chinese population. Many of the street signs are written in Chinese as well as in English

distinctive grammatical forms. Most of the first generation of Afro-Caribbeans (as black West Indians are often called) came over in the 1950s and '60s, often recruited directly by London Transport, British Rail or the National Health Service, since that was a time of rapid economic growth and a shortage of labour. But not all black immigrants arrived during those years. One who came over to England rather earlier is Martel White, who works just down the road from my house.

> No, I came to England with the army in 1941, at the age of eighteen. I was in the Artillery all through the war, right up to 1952. They wanted me to stay on, but I said no and went back to Jamaica. But life wasn't the same back home, because all my friends some gone to America, some die, some gone all over the world. So I came back here to England and joined British Telecom. Then when I come back here my Ma die and I went out to bury her; then my father die and I went out again to bury him. Then I come back.
>
> I married a Jamaican girl when I first joined the army and we started to have kids. I left her there and came over here with the army, and after two years I got a place for her to live and sent for her to come over. The first girl I had was born in Jamaica and I have five more girls all born over here. I'm not thinking of going back to Jamaica to live because my father's die, my mother's die and all my relations and friends some die and some gone away, so it don't make sense to go home. I just settle down here with my family. I have my own house in Peckham. I pay for it already, all I have to do now is pay the light bills, telephone bills and so on. I want to retire in eighteen months' time. I've done nineteen years with British Telecom and in eighteen months that'll bring me to 20 years and 201 days and then I'll just sit about.

Immigrants – or the children of immigrants – from Asia and the Caribbean stand out, literally, from the typical

British crowd. This means that, in the popular mind, immigration is associated with the fairly recent arrival of people of non-European origin. This is nonsense, of course; Britain, over the centuries, has attracted a steady stream of people from all quarters, many making the journey to find a better life for themselves and their families. That was the case of one of my neighbours, a widow called Eileen, who still speaks with the accent of her youth, despite living in London for forty-two years:

> Yes, I was a young girl when I came over here, a farm girl from just outside Cork in the south of Ireland. But that wasn't much of a life, so I travelled around Ireland for a while, doing a bit of everything, domestic service, working as a child-minder. Then I came over here to earn my living. I lived in Wandsworth first when I came to London, but I've been here in Waterloo for forty years now, mostly working as a cook.

Another neighbour, Kath Manzini, has been a resident of Waterloo all her life:

> We lived in a little courtway up there when my dad first came to England from Naples. There were lots of Italians in this neighbourhood then, most of them making ice-cream. That was my dad's business. He used to make his ice-cream at home, then he had big barrows they used to push round the streets. He died in 1950 when he was eighty-odd, so he must have come over around 1880, something like that, because he told me he was twelve when he first came over. My mum had seventeen children and ten alive. She died when she was ninety-six and she'd speak a few words in English and then she'd rattle off in Italian. I never really learned to speak it. I'd understand my mum more or less, but I can't speak more than a few words now.

Others left their countries as refugees, to escape persecution or a political system that they found intolerable. Three of my friends came here for such reasons, the eldest being Edith who, with her husband Freddy, fled from Austria in March 1938 just after Hitler marched in:

> We left in the middle of the night and went to Prague. We were living in the country and the local people banded together to help us to get away. We were only one of two Jewish families living there, but everyone helped out. We could only pack what we could carry, and I had a baby in my arms, my son Peter.
>
> My parents meanwhile had left Vienna for England, then wrote to us in Prague to tell us to get out. And we arrived in Britain on the 23rd August 1939, just a week or so before the war broke out. They'd taken all our money away and we had eighteen shillings (ninety pence) between us to start our new life. Freddy was interned for a while but was released and served in the British Army throughout the war.

The parents of Anna Przylecka met in Belsen concentration camp, which was liberated by the Americans in 1945. After a few months they were allowed to settle in England:

> They didn't speak any English at all, and they brought us up just speaking Polish. I didn't learn any English until I went to school. You see, they thought at first they'd only be here a few weeks, a matter of months at the most until the communist regime was overthrown then we'd all go home to Poland.
>
> We lived in what was quite a large Polish community in Ealing, in West London. What happened was they opened a state Catholic primary school there in 1953, and masses of Polish people flocked to Ealing to be in the school catchment area. So there's quite a flourishing Polish community in Ealing even now.

Finally there's Steve, originally Istavan, whose accent is an interesting mixture of London and Welsh with traces of his native Hungarian:

> My mother and I left Budapest in 1956, when I was eleven. My dad had been killed in the uprising. All I

> spoke was Hungarian, Russian and Latin, would you believe. My mother put me in a Catholic school in Plymouth and it took me just two years to catch up with the others. Catch up with the studies, I mean. Not just learning to speak English as well as the others. And the bit of Welsh? That came from my time in the Army. Welsh regiment.

Steve, unlike Kath Manzini, has never forgotten his mother tongue. It's the language he still speaks with his mother whenever she stays with him. But he has not passed it on to his children. When I asked him if he considered himself British or Hungarian he just answered, 'Well I served eight years in the British armed forces, much of it on active service. So what do *you* think?'

Edith too, despite a strong Austrian accent, feels completely English:

> England's our home now. There's no doubt about it. Freddy and I speak German together sometimes, but it's mostly English. We sort of drift from one to the other. I never spoke German to Peter once we were in England, so he never learned it from me.

Others feel that their original language is a link with the past, with their homeland, and one which must be preserved. Anna speaks Polish with her children and reports that the elder daughter is picking it up well:

> We have a lot of family still in Poland and I'd like to feel that my children will be able to communicate with their cousins and feel part of another culture. That's very important, I think.

But even with the language as a form of bonding, it is not always easy for a child of immigrant parents, especially one educated in Britain, to be certain of his or her national identity. When Anna was younger she was adamant that she was 'Polish and only Polish':

> In fact, I felt so strongly Polish that I went to Warsaw University for a year. But that made me realise that there was a large part of me that was English, and since spending that year I've realised that I'm neither pure English or pure Polish. Both sides are very important to me and I can't reject either.

For others, such as Louis Loizides, whose Greek-Cypriot father runs a shop in the Waterloo Road, the choice of identity can be even more complex:

> My mum's not from Cyprus, she's from Spain, from Madrid; came over in 1957. My dad came over from Cyprus a year or two later and they got married in '63. I was born here and so was my sister. I speak Spanish OK, but only a few words of Greek. I get relatives of my dad coming up to me, even customers in here who are Greek, they come up to me and expect me to speak Greek, but I have to say sorry I don't understand. In fact, when I was a kid I was learning three languages at the time, English, Spanish and Greek and it was a bit confusing, so I just dropped the Greek when I was three or four. Spanish stuck more because my mother spoke it to me. My mum and dad have always spoken English together.
>
> Do I feel one hundred per cent English? It would take me hours to answer that one. Obviously, I'm British by upbringing. I was born here and brought up here, but I do feel a part of me that's Spanish and a part that's Cypriot as well.

Such mixing together of cultures can, at best, be enriching both for the individual and for society. An individual gains from speaking more than one language, from having access to different worlds, from discovering that there are different ways of looking at things. And society, too, can benefit from the cross-fertilisation of cultural contact; the history of art and literature is proof of that.

It would be hypocritical to pretend that cultural contacts can always take place without tension, however. A minority group may find that its desire to preserve traditional values may bring it in conflict with the values – or even the laws – of the majority. Children of immigrants may reject the values of their parents, or find it difficult to reconcile them with those of society as a whole. Most distressingly, the existing population can see new arrivals as a threat to their way of life, or a source of competition for jobs and housing.

But such problems are nothing new. Irish and Jewish immigrants faced prejudice in the last century; and Huguenot refugees were doubtless greeted with suspicion 400 years ago. What is certain is that the successive and continuing waves of immigration into the great capital cities of the world make them more exciting places both to live in and to visit.

Part 4: London Changes

My part of London, Waterloo, used to be a bustling working-class area with some 30,000 inhabitants, many of them working in the factories, breweries and wharves that lined the river bank between Westminster and Blackfriars Bridges. But some of the streets and factories were bombed during the war, and others were pulled down to make space for the Festival of Britain site in 1951. Now there are fewer than 4,000 people living here, many – in my immediate area - being middle-class newcomers, happy to own houses within walking distance of the West End and City.

The older inhabitants tend to remember the pre-war neighbourhood with nostalgia. 'I'll say there's been some changes,' said one neighbour:

> Streets have gone, they've got different names. When I was a kid – and I'm eighty-nine now – there was no traffic on the road in a street like ours; just a horse and cart now and again. You could play football or cricket in the street until the copper [= policeman] came along, then you'd run. And you could go out to the shops without locking your door; no fear of anyone going in or anything like that. Your neighbours next door would always look after you. There's no such thing as neighbours nowadays. They're not friendly like they used to be years ago. If you were in trouble you'd have next-door to look after you. Everybody knew everybody else. Your sister would live down the street and your mum and dad round the corner. If a stranger came round people would notice him and ask what he was after.

And that set all the others off:

> Yes, that's right. Years ago you could knock on someone's door and say, 'Have you got a bit of salt?' or a bit of sugar, and they'd give it to you. But now you don't know people. When the old people die off they sell the house to people from outside who keep themselves to themselves. They don't even say 'good morning' to you half the time.
>
> Remember we used to call Roupell Street 'the white curtain street', it was so clean? Everyone used to see who had the nicest net curtains. And all the women used to scrub the bit of pavement in front of their door.
>
> And the market in The Cut; that used to be open till 9 o'clock on a Saturday night. If you hadn't got much money you'd wait till 8 o'clock before you went out and got your meat, because they sold it off cheap. You'd get a nice bit of beef for about 1/6d (seven pence). Yes, the market used to stretch from Waterloo Road right down to Blackfriars Road. But now they only think about the commuters. Two o'clock they're packing up and they won't serve you. They don't do things for the locals now. It's all the commuters.

And no doubt they would have carried on for hours in the same way if Tom Wilkins hadn't come along; born in 1897, served in both World Wars and old enough to remember Queen Victoria's funeral. He must have a few memories of the good old days, they said:

> Good old days? Don't talk to me about the good old days. My father was in and out of work. We'd wait for the fish-stall to close and get some fish heads or conger eel heads. There was no labour exchange, no national health. When my first kid was born the wife was ill, with pneumonia, and we had to get the district nurse in to come and see her. We never had a penny to put in the gas meter for hot water for her.

This, of course, jogged a few memories. And the women I'd

been talking to up till then starting competing with each other to recall how *bad* things had been:

> Remember the smogs? Thank God we don't have them now. They used to make everything so dirty, didn't they, the coal fires?
>
> And the steam trains! Yes, I can remember my sister Doris, she walked through the square here one day to come to see me, she had a new dress on and by the time she got here she had big black streaks all down her.
>
> And you never went to the dentist, did you? Only to get your teeth pulled out. How much was it, Mary? A penny, wasn't it?
>
> Yes, down Waterloo Road. They'd pull your teeth out with pincers for a penny when I was a kid. I'm eighty-two so that's how I know. Yes, I can remember standing outside there for two or three hours one day crying, trying to pluck up courage to go in!

Many people seem to think that changes, whether for better or worse, are inevitable, resulting from forces over which the ordinary citizen has no control. 'They' make the decisions and 'we' have to live with the consequences. But people are beginning to realise that the community can, and indeed should, unite to resist unwelcome changes.

In my own area, for example, community action prevented the building of a monster double wall of office blocks on the Coin Street site just behind the National Theatre. But this does not mean we can relax. Waterloo Station has been chosen as a Channel Tunnel terminal, which has led to property companies buying up small family businesses, hoping to build tourist shops and hotels, of little benefit to the local people; other developers have their eyes on Jubilee Gardens, one of the few remaining open spaces on the South Bank; and so it goes.

Even more developments are taking place farther downstream, in the old docklands. Since the ships stopped coming right up to London a few years ago, areas such as

LONDON
DENTIST

Bermondsey, where Lil Patrick lives, have seen massive changes:

> In the old days this was a thriving industrial area. There were lots of factories, because the raw materials came right in here by water. Lots of food came in for example, and the canning industry practically started in this area. You used to have all the different smells from the warehouses and the factories; biscuit smells from the biscuit factories, glue smells from the glue factories, jam smells from the jam factories; you'd even know what jam they were making on a given day from the smell; then there were the spices, the smells from the skins, because there was a huge tanning industry here.
>
> But there aren't any jobs now, not for the locals anyway. The only jobs we have now are the tiny one-man, self-help things. And when the industries moved out twenty-odd years ago the younger people moved out with them, so there's hardly anybody in the area in the middle-age group, say between forty-five and sixty. You've got a few younger ones with babies and infants and the rest is an ageing population. The destruction in the area has been greater than in the Blitz. This is our second Blitz, as far as I can see.
>
> Any improvement? Not for us locals, anyway. We managed to snatch back one bit of open space for the community, Potters Fields; we fought very hard for that. And we had one real victory over Coin Street; fifty-six homes that wouldn't be there if we hadn't fought for them.
>
> I've been a member of our Community Development Group since its inception in 1972 and we've been involved in fighting ever since. I'm seventy-one and I'm still fighting. I'm fourth generation in this area. My roots go too far down for me to move. I'm concerned for the area and I shall go on fighting for our rights until I can't move any more.

But fighting is sometimes of little use. More than 100,000

people are expected to work in Canary Wharf – the biggest development in Docklands – and the Government believed this venture to be so important that they allowed it to go ahead without the need for detailed planning permission. This meant that individuals and groups opposed to the new development had no official outlet for their protests.

A friend of mine, an American architect working on the final plans, gave us some idea of the scale of the operation.

> You have to realise what Canary Wharf is. What we're doing is building a new city designed on paper in Chicago. Those people didn't come to London and look at what it was like; they sat in Chicago, designed Canary Wharf, flew the drawings over here and said, 'build it'.
>
> It's a kind of travesty. Here we are building Chicago in the middle of Docklands. I just don't think it's appropriate. If they had flown over here and sat in the middle of London and then designed it, then it might have been different, but they don't care what London is.

Another friend, who worked for the post office in Docklands over three separate Christmases, was able to see how quickly the area was transformed.

> The first year it was still undeveloped, working-class flats and houses, all broken-down warehouses with just a few yuppies beginning to come in and do them up. The next year there was quite a lot of demolition and building going on, things like the Daily Telegraph building going up, all kinds of glass monstrosities. And then in 1986-87 there were new buildings everywhere you looked, all irregular shapes and different sizes, everything happening at the speed of light; you could literally see a floor going up in a couple of days.
>
> All the old council estates were now backing onto huge service industry buildings. And now if you go into that big estate, what's it called, in Limehouse, they're knocking it down to put the Docklands Highway through it. Lots of locals are quite angry about it.

According to the London Dockland Development Council there is no reason for such anger. They claim that:

> The regeneration of London Docklands is one of the most spectacular development programmes in the world today. Not only does it offer unique opportunities for business, investors and residents, it also demonstrates the importance of establishing close working relationships between a large number of different organisations, ranging from local authorities to local communities, each with their own objectives, but all with the common goal of ensuring that regeneration is a success, that it can be shared and enjoyed by all.

But not all local organisations agree. As far back as 1985, the Docklands Consultative Committee was claiming that:

> Democracy over planning is a dead letter. Decisions are taken in secret and developments given the go-ahead with only cursory scrutiny. Thus we have witnessed the absurd situation where the models and plans for the giant Hays Wharf Scheme were put on view in Switzerland before anyone in this country saw them, and permission was then rushed through by the Government using special powers it had created to overrule any objections from local authorities or Londoners. The LDDC is very far from a success story. Private development has been brought in at a price both to the taxpayer and to democracy.

Three years later the Docklands Forum, an organisation of community groups, was expressing concern about the number of houses being compulsorily purchased in order to make room for the new Docklands Highway. The eventual result, they think, 'will be the destruction of a community which had established itself over many years. It seems to prove local people's fears that there is no place for local people in a "regenerated Docklands".'

People living outside the Docklands area are not always so concerned about what is going on. One person I spoke to is confident that:

Butler's Wharf is one of the areas in the London Docklands to have been redeveloped and is now home to many young urban professional people (yuppies)

> The 1990s are going to be an exciting time. Not everyone likes it, of course, but I think a city like London has to change with the times and if the area can be made prosperous instead of being derelict, that must be all to the good.

Another one agrees, but with a certain reservation, no doubt expressing an opinion shared by many Londoners:

> It's better seeing the wharves done up and people living in them than having them all falling down. Mind you, there's a lot of money being made, and the local people aren't getting much out of it. But it's a shame seeing the old docks go. It used to be so busy and such a beautiful sight with all the ships up and down all the time. Still, that's progress, I suppose.

Exercises

Part 1: London Past

1 When did 'Londinium' first start to develop?
2 What division developed in the city under the Normans?
3 Why did London become so overcrowded?
4 Why and when did the city have to be rebuilt?
5 How did many of the streets get their names?
6 What were conditions like for the poor of the eighteenth century?
7 Who were the 'watermen', and how were they affected by development?
8 What difference developed between the north and south banks of the river?
9 What was the main influence on development in the nineteenth century?
10 What do you understand by the terms 'urban sprawl' and 'green belt'?
11 What was the effect of the 'Blitz' in the 1940s?
12 How has the city skyline changed since the Second World War?

Part 2: London Pleasures

13 How would you like to spend a day in London? Write down where you would go and what you would do from the range of suggestions in Part Two.

Part 3: London People

14 What sort of people are 'Londoners' nowadays?
15 How does the changing face of a building on the

corner of Fournier Street and Brick Lane reflect the history of immigration in the East End?
16 What business has been taken up by the majority of (a) Gujarati Asians? (b) Chinese?
17 What difficulties do children of immigrant parents face?

Part 4: London Changes
18 What aspects of the past do some Londoners feel nostalgic about?
19 What things do they *not* miss?
20 What role are community action groups beginning to play?
21 Why is Canary Wharf significant?
22 What mixed feelings do Londoners express about the new Docklands development?

Glossary

PAGE

7 ***Act*** (n): law passed by government
'. . . the famous 1710 Act for the Building of Fifty Churches.'

44 ***adamant*** (adj): be unwilling to change your mind about something
'She was adamant that she was 'Polish and only Polish'.'

25 ***adjacent*** (adj): next to
'. . . you have reduced entry to the adjacent Museum . . .'

10 ***alley*** (n): narrow street between buildings
'. . . the courts and alleys off St Martin's Lane.'

1 ***amphitheatre*** (n): ancient Roman-style theatre
'. . . began a major rebuilding programme, including an amphitheatre . . .'

35 ***ancestry*** (n): line of parents, grandparents, etc. back in time
'. . . or can trace their ancestry back considerably earlier.'

41 ***Artillery*** (n): part of army trained to use big, powerful guns
'I was in the Artillery all through the war . . .'

16 ***attendant*** (n): person whose job is to help/serve people, eg in museum, art gallery, shop, petrol station, etc.

'. . . don't run or the attendants will be very worried.'

37 ***bagel*** (n): doughnut-shaped (round) bread roll (Jewish)

'. . . the cheesecake and bagels . . . '

16 ***barge*** (n): boat with flat bottom

'Henry travelled in the royal barge . . .'

7 ***baroque*** (adj): ornate, decorative style popular in Europe in seventeenth and eighteenth centuries

'. . . one of the few truly baroque squares in London.'

13 ***Blitz*** (n): term given to heavy bombing of London/ British cities during Second World War

'Night after night for months on end, the 'Blitz' went on.'

44 ***bonding*** (n): joining together; forming close relationships

'But even with the language as a form of bonding . . . '

18 ***bric-a-brac*** (n): small, cheap ornaments

'There is everything from cheap clothes to bric-a-brac and antiques.'

47 ***brewery*** (n): place where beer is made

'. . . the factories, breweries and wharves that lined the river bank . . . '

5 ***brothel*** (n): place men visit and pay to have sex with prostitutes

'. . . there were inns and brothels . . . '

47 ***bustling*** (adj): busy, with lots of activity

'Waterloo used to be a bustling working-class area . . . '

52 ***canning industry***: business of putting food into tins/ cans

'. . . the canning industry practically started in this area.'

43 ***catchment area*** (n): area covered/served by school (or hospital, etc.)
' . . . Polish people flocked to Ealing to be in the school catchment area.'

39 ***catering*** (n): providing food/drink
'An astonishing ninety per cent of the estimated 100,000 Chinese living in Britain are in the catering industry.'

22 ***chapel*** (n): small church
'The chapel is said to have been rebuilt by Inigo Jones . . . '

42 ***child-minder***: person whose job is to look after someone else's children (often while parents are at work)
' . . . working as a child-minder.'

54 ***compulsorily*** (adv): forcibly (as part of the law); without choice
' . . . concern about the number of houses being compulsorily purchased . . . '

38 ***contractor*** (n): person who does particular jobs (eg building) for others
' . . . rapidly becoming one of the top contractors in the country.'

3 ***convent*** (n): place where nuns (religious women) stay
'In and around the City were dozens of monasteries and convents . . . '

10 ***court*** (n): (courtyard) flat, paved area surrounded by buildings
' . . . the courts and alleys off St Martin's Lane . . . '

42 ***courtway*** (n): (see ***court*** above)

5 ***cram*** (v): push too many people/things into small space
' . . . people were crammed into each room . . . '

54 ***cursory*** (adj): quick, without paying careful attention
' . . . and developments given the go-ahead with only cursory scrutiny.'

10 ***dead*** (adj): completely
' . . . dead drunk for tuppence.'

54 ***dead letter*** (n): a law that is made but not carried out properly
'Democracy over planning is a dead letter.'

15 ***deplorably*** (adv): very wrongly; hopelessly
' . . . the 'deplorably low standard' of what was being built . . . '

56 ***derelict*** (adj): ruined; unused and in need of repair
' . . . the area can be made prosperous instead of being derelict . . . '

53 ***do up*** (v): repair, decorate, modernise
' . . . with just a few yuppies beginning to come in and do them up.'

15 ***drabness*** (n): dullness, being without interest
'In 1959, the Royal Fine Art Commission referred to the 'drabness' . . . of much modern inner-city architecture . . . '

5 ***Elizabethan*** (adj): from the period of Queen Elizabeth I (1533–1603) or her reign (1558–1603)
'But it was here, too, that the great Elizabethan theatres were to be found.'

27 ***ethnographic*** (adj): relating to the study of different cultures/races
' . . . its ethnographic department, **The Museum of Mankind** . . . '

2 ***excavations*** (n): digging to find information about/articles from the past
' . . . recent excavations have uncovered a complete Roman waterfront.'

38 ***firm*** (n): company; business
'Within ten years he had founded his own firm . . .'

32 ***flea-market*** (n): market selling cheap second-hand clothes/goods
' . . . just off Brick Lane, is the oldest flea market in London.'

37 ***flee*** (v): run away from/escape hurriedly
' . . . fleeing religious persecution . . . '

43 ***flock*** (v): move together in large groups (usually when attracted by something)
' . . . masses of Polish people flocked to Ealing . . .'

38 ***foreman*** (n): person in charge of a group of workers
'His father . . . started work in 1946 as a foreman for a building firm in Kenya.'

1 ***fortification*** (n): building used as protection against attack
' . . . they started building on the north bank, probably using the twin hills of St Paul's and Cornhill for the first fortifications.'

38 ***found*** (v): start; set up
'Within ten years he had founded his own firm . . . '

29 ***foyer*** (n): open area just inside entrance to theatre, hotel, etc.
'The Festival Hall has a programme of foyer music . . .'

35 ***furrier*** (n): person who makes or sells clothes made from animal furs
'He was a furrier . . . '

13 ***Green Belt*** (n): park/countryside area where no building is allowed
' . . . the London County Council proposed a 'Green Belt' area around London . . . '

17 ***heron*** (n): bird with very long legs and long beak
'Herons still sit on the branches of the trees watching for fish . . . '

33 ***hot*** (adj): spicy (giving hot/burning feeling in the mouth)
'The menu will normally say how 'hot' a dish is.'

45 ***hypocritical*** (adj): pretending to be something it is not; false behaviour
'It would be hypocritical to pretend that cultural contacts can always take place without tension.'

30 ***interactive*** (adj): computer and user can communicate with each other directly (using keyboard)
' . . . excellent exhibits with interactive video display.'

52 ***inception*** (n): beginning; founding
'I've been a member of our Community Development Group since its inception in 1972 . . .'

43 ***intern*** (v): keep someone prisoner (often for political reasons)
'Freddy was interned for a while . . . '

22 ***Knights Templar***: a religious and military order of men who fought to protect Christianity
'This was originally the headquarters of the Knights Templar until they were abolished in 1312.'

37 ***kosher*** (adj): approved by Jewish law (eg for food)
' . . . with the best kosher food in London.'

49 ***labour exchange*** (n): place where unemployed people register (and collect money from government)
'There was no labour exchange . . . '

20 ***longitude (line of)***: position on world map with reference to set vertical line
'The zero line of longitude runs through the grounds . . . '

21 ***maritime*** (adj): to do with the sea
'Below the Observatory is the National Maritime Museum . . . '

1 ***marshy*** (adj): wet and muddy
'The south bank was flat and marshy then . . . '

29 ***matinee*** (n): afternoon performance (in the theatre or cinema)
'12.00pm–1.30pm for matinees.'

15 ***mediocrity*** (n): without imagination; not particularly good or bad
' . . . the 'drabness' and 'mediocrity' of much modern inner-city architecture . . . '

6 ***mews*** (n): stables; building (in a street) where horses are kept
' . . . horses and carriages could be kept in the private 'mews' running behind the houses.'

3 ***monastery*** (n): place where community of monks (religious men) live
'In and around the City were dozens of monasteries and convents . . . '

47 ***nostalgia*** (n): a feeling of affection and longing for the past
'The older inhabitants tend to remember the prewar neighbourhood with nostalgia.'

22 ***oasis*** (n): pleasant/safe place surrounded by unpleasant ones
'The Temple is an oasis of peace and quiet . . . '

37 ***persecution*** (n): cruel, unfair, dangerous treatment
' . . . fleeing religious persecution in the late seventeenth century.'

6 ***piazza*** (n): large, open square
'When it came to Covent Garden he decided to build an Italian-style piazza . . . '

50 ***pincers*** (n): instrument (something like scissors) used to hold things tightly and pull them out

'They'd pull your teeth out with pincers for a penny . . . '

37 ***precinct*** (n): area; territory

' . . . they formed, within their own precinct, an ethnic majority . . . '

46 ***prejudice*** (n): feeling of dislike or unfair treatment usually directed at people of particular race/religion

'Irish and Jewish immigrants faced prejudice in the last century.'

13 ***premises*** (n): buildings/property of business or institution

' . . . department stores and other commercial premises.'

12 ***prestigious*** (adj): important, influential, of great value

'On the other side of the river, more prestigious developments were taking place.'

10 ***prostitute*** (n): person (usually a woman) who has sex in exchange for money

'Even the wide streets such as the Haymarket were full of prostitutes . . . '

5 ***Puritans*** (n): group of English Protestants who tried to get rid of Roman Catholic influence in England

' . . . when the Puritans came to power at the time of the Civil War.'

42 ***rattle off*** (v): say something quickly, without pausing

' . . . and then she'd rattle off in Italian.'

41 ***recruit*** (v): find people to work for a particular company

' . . . often recruited directly by London Transport, British Rail or the National Health Service . . . '

42 ***refugee*** (n): person who has to leave their country, often for political reasons, to find safety elsewhere
'Others left their countries as refugees . . . '

54 ***regeneration*** (n): development that makes something more active/successful
'The regeneration of London Docklands is one of the most spectacular development programmes in the world today.'

56 ***reservation*** (n): doubt; not completely sure
'Another one agrees, but with a certain reservation . . . '

54 ***scrutiny*** (n): study; observation
' . . . and developments given the go-ahead with only cursory scrutiny.'

12 ***slum*** (adj): area of poor housing/living conditions
'Much of the central slum area was pulled down as new wide streets were built . . . '

50 ***smog*** (n): thick fog/smoke caused by pollution
'Remember the smogs?'

15 ***spire*** (n): tall, pointed part on top of church
' . . . with the spires of the other Wren churches standing out proudly.'

13 ***sprawl*** (n): covering large area untidily/without good planning
' . . . as what has been called the 'urban sprawl' carried on . . . '

25 ***standby*** (n): cheap tickets available just before an event starts
'Unsold tickets and a few 'standby' tickets are available . . . '

6 ***stock*** (v): put quantity of goods (here, animals and birds) into a place
' . . . stocking it with animals and birds.'

52 ***tanning*** (adj): making animal skins into leather
'. . . there was a huge tanning industry here.'

12 ***terraced*** (adj): row of attached houses of the same design
'. . . soon filled up with cheap, working-class terraced housing.'

52 ***thriving*** (adj): very successful, busy
'In the old days this was a thriving industrial area.'

1 ***tidal*** (adj): rising and falling in level with the sea tides
'. . . not too far from the coast and situated on a tidal river . . . '

1 ***troops*** (n): soldiers
'. . . the troops of the Emperor Claudius . . . '

53 ***travesty*** (n): bad imitation of something
'It's a kind of travesty.'

38 ***turnover*** (n): total value of things sold in a particular period
'. . . we have had little difficulty in increasing our turnover.'

21 ***upper courts*** (n): the places where judges etc. come together to deal with the more serious law cases
'. . . barristers, who appear in the upper courts . . .'

22 ***Victorian*** (adj): from the time of Queen Victoria's reign (1837–1901)
'. . . the Hall and Library are early Victorian . . .'

33 ***volunteer*** (n): someone who offers to do something (without being paid)
'. . . usually run by volunteers from the local area.'

37 ***weaving*** (n): when thread is made into cloth
'Over the next hundred years it became the centre of the silk weaving industry.'

47 ***wharf*** (n): place where goods are put onto and taken off ships
' . . . the factories, breweries and wharves that lined the river bank . . . '

53 ***yuppie*** (n): young professional person earning a lot of money and spending it freely
' . . . with just a few yuppies beginning to come in and do them up.'

Language Grading in the **Macmillan Bookshelf Series**

This reader has been written using a loosely controlled range of language structures. There is no tight control of vocabulary as it is based on the authors' experience of the kind of vocabulary range expected at each particular language level. The authors have also taken care to contextualise any unfamiliar words, which are further explained in the glossary. We hope you will try to deduce meaning from the context, and will use a dictionary where necessary to expand your lexical knowledge.

The language items listed here show those most commonly used at each level in the **Bookshelf** series:

Level One (elementary)

Mainly simple and compound sentences, beginning to use more complex sentences but with limited use of sub clauses

Present Simple
Present Continuous
(present and future reference)
Past Continuous
'Going to' future
Past Simple
(regular and a few common irregular)
Can (ability)
Would like (offer, request)
Positive and negative statements
Interrogative
Imperative
And, or, but, so, because, before, after
Some/any (-thing)
Basic adjectives
Some common adverbs
'Simple' comparatives, superlatives
Gerunds/infinitives, common verbs

Level Two (lower intermediate)

Simple and compound sentences, limited use of complex sentences

Present Perfect
Will/won't future
Present/Past Simple Passive
Have to, must, should, could
Can/may (requests/permission)
Infinitives (like, want, try, etc.)
Gerunds (start, finish, after, like, etc.)
Conditional, can, could (possibility)
When/while
Question tags, reflexives
Comparatives, superlatives
(common adjectives/adverbs)
Reported speech (present/past)

Level Three (intermediate)

More complex sentences, including embedded clauses

Present Perfect Continuous
Past Perfect
Present/Past Continuous Passives
Perfect Passives
Ought to
May/might (possibility)
Conditionals 1 and 2
Although, to/in order to, since
(reason)
So/neither
Reported statements, requests, etc.

Level Four (upper intermediate)

At this stage there is minimal control, although authors generally avoid unnecessary complexity

Future Continuous
Past Perfect Continuous
More complex passives
Conditionals 3